Discovering Cultures

Russia

Sarah De Capua

***B*ENCHMARK *B*OOKS**

MARSHALL CAVENDISH
NEW YORK

With thanks to Kevin P. Hallinan, East Central European Center, Columbia University,
for the careful review of this manuscript.

Benchmark Books
Marshall Cavendish
99 White Plains Road
Tarrytown, New York 10591-9001
www.marshallcavendish.com

Library of Congress Cataloging-in-Publication Data

De Capua, Sarah.
Russia / Sarah De Capua.
p. cm. — (Discovering cultures)
Summary: Highlights the geography, people, food, schools, recreation, celebrations, and language of Russia.
Includes bibliographical references and index.
ISBN 0-7614-1716-8
1. Russia (Federation)—Juvenile literature. [1. Russia (Federation)]
I. Title. II. Series.
DK510.23.D4 2003
947—dc21   2003006957

Photo Research by Candlepants Incorporated
Cover Photo: Andrea Jemolo / Corbis

The photographs in this book are used by permission and through the courtesy of; *Natalie B. Fobes*: 1, 22, back cover. *Corbis*: Galen Rowell, 4; Dean Conger, 7, 30, 43 (right); Wolfgang Kaehler, 8, 15, 31; AFP, 11, 29, 34; Dave G. Houser, 12 (left); Archivo Iconografico, S.A., 12 (right); Charles O'Rear, 13, 34 (top left); Yogi, Inc., 14; Steve Raymer, 16, 28; Peter Turnley, 18, 44 (left); David Turnley, 19; Robert Maass, 24; Keerle de Georges / Sygma, 26; Jacques Langevin, 32; Shepard Sherbell, 36; Dave Bartruff, 37; Sygma, 38; Bettmann, 44 (right); Hulton-Deutsch, 45. *Getty Images*: The Image Bank / Jochem D. Wijnands, 6, 42; National Geographic / Sarah Leen, 9, 43 (lower left); Stone / James Balog, 10. *Morton Beebe*: 17. *Envision*: Steven Mark Needham, 20; Vladmir Morozov, 21. *The Images Works*: Jeff Greenberg, 25; Hideo Haga / HAGA, 35. *The Bridgeman Art Library*: Archive Charmet, 27.

Cover: *St. Basil's Cathedral in Moscow*; Title page: *A young Inuit girl*

Map and illustrations by Ian Warpole
Book design by Virginia Pope

Printed in China
1 3 5 6 4 2

Turn the Pages...

Where in the World Is Russia?

The country of Russia covers two continents: Asia and Europe. Russia is 5,000 miles (8,000 kilometers) wide. It is 2,500 miles (4,000 km) from north to south. This is almost twice as big as the United States. Russia crosses eleven time zones. When people in the eastern part of the country are going to sleep, the people in the western part of the country are just sitting down to lunch.

Russia's landscape contains plains, mountains, taiga, and tundra. About 20,000 lakes and thousands of rivers make it a watery land. Lake Baikal, in south central

The Blue Bay in Siberia

Map of Russia

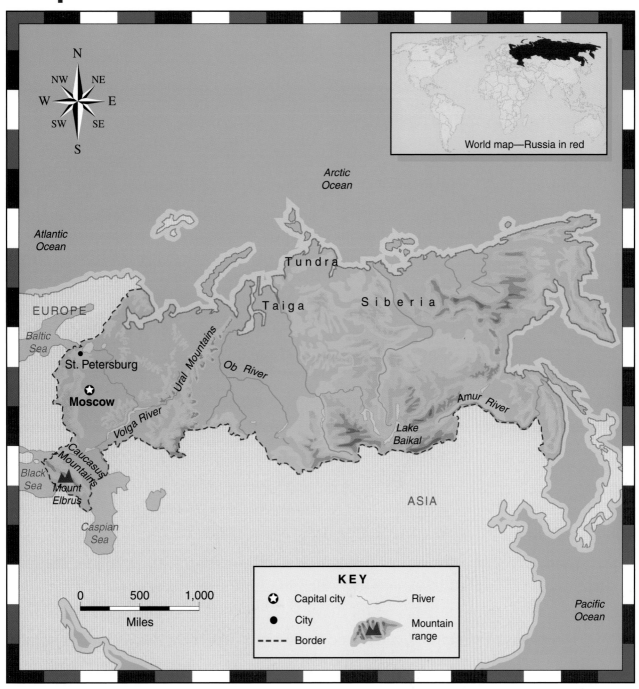

World map—Russia in red

N
NW · NE
W · E
SW · SE
S

Arctic Ocean

Atlantic Ocean

Tundra

Taiga

Siberia

EUROPE

Baltic Sea

St. Petersburg

Moscow

Ural Mountains

Ob River

Amur River

Volga River

Lake Baikal

Caucasus Mountains

Black Sea

Mount Elbrus

ASIA

Caspian Sea

Pacific Ocean

0   500   1,000
Miles

KEY

⊛ Capital city   〰 River

● City

– – – Border   ⛰ Mountain range

5

A nighttime view of Moscow, Russia's capital city

Russia, is the deepest freshwater lake in the world. It is more than a mile (1.6 km) deep. This lake covers about 12,200 square miles (31,600 sq km).

Water surrounds Russia. The Arctic Ocean lies to the north. The Pacific Ocean is to the east. The Baltic Sea and the Atlantic Ocean can be reached through the city of St. Petersburg. Russia's major rivers include the Amur, Ob, and Volga.

The plains of western Russia are covered with grass and forests. Russia's largest cities, St. Petersburg and Moscow, are found here. Moscow is the capital of Russia.

The peak of Mount Elbrus is always snow-covered.

The Caucasus Mountains are in the southwest, between the Black and Caspian Seas. Mount Elbrus is Russia's highest peak. It is 18,465 feet (5,628 meters) high. The Ural Mountains separate Europe and Asia. These mountains also divide western Russia from Siberia, the eastern part of Russia.

Siberia is a huge region that is mostly a plateau. A plateau is an area of high, flat land. Thick forests and huge grasslands grow in Siberia. Mountains cover parts of the region, especially in the south and east. Some mountains jut into the Pacific Ocean. They form *peninsulas*. The best-known peninsula is the Kamchatka. It is called "the land of fire and ice." The Kamchatka is mostly snow-covered, but hot springs and *geysers* are also found here. While most of Siberia is frozen and covered with snow, places in south central Siberia can be very hot in summer.

The taiga region of Siberia

The tundra is found in the far north. It is a frozen region along the Arctic Ocean. No trees grow in the tundra. Even during the summer, the ground is frozen. Only the top few inches of the soil thaw enough for small shrubs, grasses, and plants to grow.

The world's largest forest grows south of the tundra. This region is called the taiga. Evergreen trees, such as fir and pine, are the most common trees in the taiga.

Russia's huge size means that thousands of different animals can live there. Fish and sea animals, such as seals, swim in the water. Birds, including crows, magpies, and sparrows, fly through the sky. Brown bears, wolves, foxes, hedgehogs, and hares roam the forests. Polar bears, walrus, and reindeer live in the north. Siberian tigers, the world's largest cats, are found in the cold eastern mountains.

The Brown Bear

The brown bear is Russia's national animal. Brown bears live in the mountains throughout the country. Males grow up to 9 feet (274 centimeters) tall and weigh 800 pounds (363 kilograms). Females are about 7 feet (213 cm) tall and weigh 700 pounds (318 kg). All brown bears have a hump on their shoulders and long, curved claws. They eat fish, squirrels, berries, grasses, and the roots of some plants. They have good hearing and excellent eyesight. They can smell something from more than a mile (1.6 km) away. Brown bears walk slowly, but if threatened they can run 30 miles (48 km) an hour!

During Russia's long winters, brown bears do not really hibernate. Hibernation is a deep sleep that lasts for months. Brown bears go into a sleep similar to hibernation, but they can wake up if they sense danger.

Brown bears are very strong, smart, and quick. When angry, they act courageously—especially if a mother bear is protecting her cubs. This makes it easy to see why Russians chose the brown bear as their national animal.

What Makes Russia Russian?

The people of Russia are as different as the land. More than 80 ethnic groups make Russia home. Most of Russia's 145 million people live in the western part of the country.

These Russian children are from many different ethnic groups.

Russia's official name is the Russian Federation. It is a *democracy*. Russia is made up of eighty-nine regions. Voters in each region elect representatives to the government. Russians also vote for their nation's president and for local government leaders.

Russian is the official language of Russia. People from other countries who live in Russia may also speak their own languages. Russian is written in the Cyrillic alphabet, which has thirty-two letters. The Roman alphabet, which Americans use, has only twenty-six letters. The Cyrillic alphabet has letters that are written and pronounced differently than the English alphabet.

Russia's main religion is Russian Orthodox, a branch of Christianity. The Russian Orthodox Church follows a different calendar from other Christian churches. For example, Christmas is celebrated on January 7. New Year's is January 13.

Russian music and dance is famous throughout the world. Russian composers have worked with international symphonies and operas. Russian ballet dancers are believed to be the best in the world. Visitors from many countries come to see the Bolshoi Ballet of Moscow and the Kirov Ballet of St. Petersburg.

A performance by members of the Bolshoi Ballet

A folk musician playing a balalaika

Icons are common in Russian Orthodox churches.

Folk music and dance are performed throughout the country. The *balalaika* is a three-stringed instrument. It is similar to a guitar. The balalaika is played in villages and folk bands.

Museums throughout Russia display the works of Russian artists. The best-known Russian paintings are called icons. Icons are religious pictures painted on wood panels by artists in the Russian Orthodox Church. Icons can be seen in the churches, as well as the famous Hermitage Museum in St. Petersburg.

Russian novels, plays, and movies have been translated into many different languages. The novelist Alexander Solzhenitsyn won the Nobel Prize for Literature in 1970.

Architecture is the style in which buildings are made. Russian architecture is famous all over the world. For hundreds of years, onion-shaped domes, some of

A full moon rises over St. Basil's Cathedral in Moscow.

Brightly decorated matrioshka dolls

which are covered in gold, have topped many of Russia's buildings. Two famous examples of these beautiful domes are on St. Basil's Cathedral in Moscow and Kizhi Island Church in northern Russia. No one is quite sure how the onion shape came to be. Some people think it was developed because snow slides off it easily.

Do you know someone who collects *matrioshka* dolls? Matrioshka is Russian for little woman. These colorfully painted dolls are made of wood. Each doll in a set of six or seven is smaller than the one before it. One doll stacks inside another until all of the dolls are stacked inside the biggest one. Visitors to Russia often purchase matrioshka dolls.

Traditional Dress

Russians are so different that there are hundreds of styles of traditional dress. Regions and villages often follow their own fashions.

The Inuit live in northern Russia, where it is very cold. The Inuit wear fur clothing, including shoes. The temperatures go down to -100 degrees Fahrenheit (-73 degrees Celsius). It is very important for the people who live in this region to dress warmly.

In warmer areas, farmers wear light shirts with decorated collars, cuffs, and hems. Long ago, these decorations were believed to protect people from evil spirits.

Traditional clothing tells a lot about the people who wear it. Details about the group's history, the climate they live in, and the work they do can be identified by the clothes they wear.

Living in Russia

There are many differences between the way people live in the city and the way they live in the country. Russian cities look like cities in North America. However, the skyscrapers are not as tall and public transportation has more problems. Most people live in apartment buildings. They dress like people in North American cities. Men wear jackets, pants, shirts, and ties. Women wear dresses or blouses with skirts or pants.

Most people who live in the city work Monday through Friday. Some may work for the government. Others may

St. Petersburg is one of Russia's largest cities.

This fountain in Moscow is a popular place to meet friends.

work in factories where they make cars, shoes, or electronics. Saturdays and Sundays are their days off. They might spend their weekends at parks, theaters, museums, restaurants, or sports stadiums.

Farmers live in the country in homes made of wood and brick. Their way of life is not as modern as life in the city. Many houses do not have electricity or running water. The nearest neighbor may be many miles away.

Russian farmers on the plains grow wheat, corn, and sunflowers. Rice, soybeans, and sugar beets are grown in the south. Near the Black Sea, farmers grow tea and fruits. In the taiga, farmers raise dairy cattle and grow potatoes. On the tundra, people fish or hunt reindeer to feed their families. In the country, people usually work seven days a week. Farmers take time off to attend church services on Saturday evening or Sunday morning. They also travel to neighbors' homes for friendly visits.

An old Russian saying goes, "No dinner without bread." Nearly every Russian meal begins with rye bread. Breakfast is usually rye bread, cheese, and tea. Homemade raspberry, strawberry, apple, or pear jam is used to sweeten the tea, instead of sugar.

Dinner is the main meal. It is eaten in the middle of the day, like lunch. Dinner is usually a meat dish—beef, chicken, fish,

Bread is a part of most Russian meals.

Farmworkers picking tomatoes

Borscht is often served with a spoonful of sour cream.

or pork—with potatoes and other vegetables, such as beets or cabbage. Mushrooms are a favorite at Russian meals. They are grown throughout the country, and are fried, pickled, salted, or boiled.

Supper is eaten in the late evening. It usually involves another meat dish. Homemade *schi* (cabbage soup) and *solyanka*, a soup made with different kinds of meat or fish, are popular. *Borscht* (beet soup) comes from Russia. Russians also like *pelmeni*, small meat pies boiled in water. They are similar to beef ravioli.

One of the most popular drinks in Russia is *kvass*. Kvass is made of brown bread or malted rye flour. It is a refreshing drink on hot summer days. Kvass is sometimes added to chopped meat and vegetables to make *okroshka*, a cold soup.

Russian desserts are usually cakes, fresh fruits, candies, or spice cakes. Russian spice cakes are buns with honey and spices, covered with sweet syrup. Nearly every Russian home includes a samovar. A samovar is an urn in which water is boiled to make tea. Hot water comes from a spout at the bottom of the samovar and fills a teapot. The teapot is then placed on top of the samovar to stay hot.

A samovar holds hot water for the tea that will be served with this cake.

Tea is a popular drink in Russia.

Meals differ among Russian ethnic groups. For example, the people of the north eat mutton (sheep's meat) and fish. These dishes are usually served raw, as are the fat and blood of reindeer, seal, or whale. *Stroganina* is made of thinly sliced meat or fish spiced with salt, roots, and berries. Reindeer milk and hot tea are also common.

Let's Eat!
Russian Teacakes

Ask an adult to help you prepare these tasty Russian treats.

Ingredients:

1 cup butter, softened

1 teaspoon vanilla

2 1/2 cups flour

3 tablespoons sugar

1 1/2 cups confectioner's sugar

1/2 cup walnuts, finely chopped

1 teaspoon baking powder

dash salt

Wash your hands before you begin. Preheat the oven to 350 degrees Fahrenheit (177 degrees Celsius). Mix butter, sugar, baking powder, and vanilla thoroughly. Slowly add flour, salt, and nuts and mix with your hands until the dough holds together. If needed, add more flour, so it does not stick to your hands. Shape dough into one-inch balls. Place on an ungreased baking sheet. Bake for 10 to 15 minutes, but do not brown. While the cakes are still warm, roll each very well in confectioner's sugar. Cool the cakes and roll again in confectioner's sugar. Serve with tea.

School Days

All Russian children must attend school from ages six to seventeen. Education is free in Russia. Some parents send their children to schools that are like private schools in the United States. They must pay for these schools. Children as young as five can go to preschool. There they learn to read, write, and count. They also play games and do outdoor activities.

Russian schoolchildren

Some Russian schoolchildren wear uniforms to school. Boys usually have a navy jacket and pants, with a white shirt. Girls wear navy skirts and white shirts. Russian children attend school five days a week, from Monday through Friday. The school day begins at about 8 A.M. and ends at about 3 P.M. Some children participate in after-school sports or programs until 6:00 P.M.

Each school year starts on September 1 and ends in mid-June. Students have time off in the fall and spring, and during Russian Orthodox Christmastime. After the school year ends in June, each student must spend two weeks helping out at the school. Jobs include painting classrooms, cleaning, making repairs, washing windows, and organizing the library. Summer vacation takes place in July and August.

When children start school, they are put into classes of twenty-five to thirty students. These classes do not change for the entire eleven years of school. Students study mathematics, literature, social studies, history, geography, and Russian. They learn two foreign languages, as well. English is the most popular, but French, Spanish, or German are studied too. A child's school day also includes classes in music, art, and physical education. Many schools have computers in the classrooms.

Students in an art class

An elementary school classroom in Russia

Some students attend special schools to study computers, math, and sciences, including algebra, physics, and chemistry. Other students go to schools that focus on art, music, languages, or electronics. There are even schools that prepare students for work in places like factories.

Some students continue their education at a Russian college or university. Many attend universities in other countries, such as the United States.

Baba Yaga

Russian schoolchildren love folktales about Baba Yaga. Baba Yaga is an ugly witch with iron teeth who flies through the air in a *mortar* and *pestle*. She carries a broom to sweep away traces of her travels. Baba Yaga lives in a hut in a dark forest. The hut spins around on top of chicken legs. Her hut is surrounded by a fence made of the bones of the people she has eaten. On top of the fence are their skulls.

Although most Baba Yaga stories describe her as mean and scary, in other stories she is wise and helpful. In parts of Russia, she is called Baba Yaga Kostianaya Noga (Baba Yaga Boney Legs) because she is as thin as a skeleton.

Children and adults enjoy the tales of Baba Yaga because they always teach a good lesson.

Just for Fun

Russians love to be outside, even in this land of long, dark winters. Children can be found ice-skating, sledding, or playing ice hockey. Adults can be seen bundled up against the cold sipping hot tea or chocolate at outdoor cafés. Many go ice fishing or cross-country skiing.

Wintertime fun on a snowy day

Playing ice hockey on a frozen pond

It is not always cold and snowy in Russia. Most Russians go on vacation each year, usually in the summer. The most popular vacation spots are Moscow and resorts on the Black Sea. At resorts and lakesides, Russians enjoy swimming and boating. Another popular place to vacation is the *dacha*. A dacha is a home in the country.

Swimming in the Black Sea in the summer

It may be a tiny cottage or a large house. At the dacha, adults walk, garden, fish, or swim. Children swim and play in the warm sunshine.

Inside or out, the most popular game in Russia is chess. Russians of all ages enjoy chess. Outdoor chess games in local parks or on street corners are common. Russia is home to many world-champion chess players. Stamp collecting is another popular hobby for young and old. Thousands of stamp clubs have been established throughout the country.

A dacha and garden in the Russian countryside

Russians get much of their news and entertainment from cable and satellite television. Many of the same programs seen in North America are shown on Russian television. In cities, families visit theaters and museums. Russians also enjoy a wide variety of books, magazines, and newspapers.

Sports are an important part of Russian life. Gyms, indoor swimming pools, and stadiums are used every day. Thousands of people participate in basketball and volleyball games, as well as gymnastics and track-and-field events. Soccer, however, is by far the most popular sport in Russia. From local children's teams to their national team, Russians rarely miss a soccer match!

Some Russians have their own traditional sports. In central Siberia, for exam-ple, the Yakut have reindeer-sled races. The Buryat of eastern Siberia enjoy archery. In this sport, people shoot at targets using a bow and arrow.

A reindeer-sled race in Siberia

Shitalka (Counting)

This game is similar to the North American game of hide-and-seek. It can be played with any number of children. The children pick someone to be "It." That child counts to twenty-five, while the other players run and hide. After the child who is It has finished counting, he or she shouts, "Everyone should hide because I am going to find you!" When the child who is It finds players in their hiding places, those players have to pay him a fine. The fine is not money. It can be candy, gum, marbles, or anything the children have decided. The child who is It finds as many players as possible. If he finds them all, that child is It again. Whoever is not found comes out after all the fines have been paid and then that child becomes It. At the end of the game, whoever has collected the most fines is the winner.

Let's Celebrate!

Russian festivals and holidays are times to share good food and fun with family and friends.

Russian birthdays are celebrated like birthdays in North America. There are par-ties, presents, food, music, and games. A birthday cake with candles on top is served. Some Russians prefer to eat birthday pie instead of birthday cake. The happy birthday greeting is carved into the crust.

An Ice Festival is held throughout Russia during the winter. Huge buildings made entirely of ice are carved in city parks. Many do not melt until spring.

Christmas comes to Russia on January 7. It is not celebrated as widely as it is in North America. Everyone has the day off from work

Carving ice sculptures for the Ice Festival

Russians dressed as Grandfather Frost and Snow Maiden

or school. Some people attend church services. January is the coldest month in Russia, so snow is likely to cover the ground almost everywhere. Children spend this holiday playing in the snow.

New Year's is the biggest holiday in Russia. Many Russians celebrate it twice— once on January 1, and again on January 13. New Year's is celebrated like Christmas in the United States. Grandfather Frost and his granddaughter, Snow

Celebrating New Year's with fireworks in Moscow

Maiden, give out presents. On New Year's Eve, families gather around a decorated evergreen tree to eat a large meal and exchange gifts.

February 23 is Soldier's Day. It is a holiday for all men. It is celebrated like Father's Day in the United States. Women have their day on March 8. It is called Women's Day. It is like Mother's Day in the United States. On this day, men give women gifts and flowers. Many men also do all the chores around the house on Women's Day.

Painted Easter eggs

Easter comes in spring. The exact date changes from year to year. People attend church services and paint eggs. They enjoy *kulich* (Easter cake) and *pashka* (a dish made with curd cheese) all day long with families and friends.

In different parts of the country, celebrations are held in spring to mark the planting of crops. During the celebrations, farmers give presents to children. Games such as the egg-and-spoon race, the three-legged race, running, and wrestling take place. In some areas, people sing songs that honor nature. They parade through the streets with flowers.

Victory Day is May 9. It marks the day World War II (1939–1945) ended. Parades are held in Moscow and other cities. Fireworks explode over Moscow. Wreaths are laid at the graves of Russians who died serving their country in both World War I (1914–1918) and World War II.

June 12 is Russia's newest holiday, Independence Day. For more than seventy years, Russia was a communist country. The government owned all of the country's

A military parade on Victory Day in Moscow

goods, property, and businesses. But on June 12, 1991, the Declaration of Sovereignty of the Russian Federation was adopted. This declaration meant that the communist Soviet Union, which included Russia and many other smaller countries, no longer existed. Russia became an independent country.

National Day is celebrated on November 7. It marks the day of the 1917 revolution. This revolution ended Russia's rule by emperors called *czars*. The communist government was set up at that time. Although Russia is no longer a communist country, the day is celebrated in many areas with military parades.

A New Year's Song

This is a traditional song that children also recite as a poem:

In the woods was born an evergreen tree
In summer and winter it was straight and green.
The snow sang it a lullaby:
"Sleep, evergreen tree, sleep tight!"
The frost put snow around it saying, "Don't freeze!"
The rabbit hopped under it; the angry wolf just ran by.
An old man came and chopped it down
And now you are our beautifully decorated
New Year's tree.

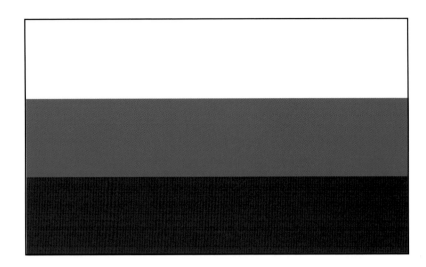

The Russian flag is made up of three wide stripes: white on top, blue in the middle, and red on the bottom. The white stripe stands for goodness and openness. The blue stripe stands for honesty and faithfulness to the country. The red stripe stands for courage, generosity, and love.

The ruble is Russia's form of money. One hundred kopecks equal one ruble. In 2003, you could get 30 rubles for one U.S. dollar.

Count in Russian

English	Russian	Say it like this:
one	odin	au-DEEN
two	dva	da-VAH
three	tre	TREE
four	chetery	che-TEARY
five	pyat	PYAHT
six	shest	SHAYST
seven	sem	SEM
eight	vosem	VOH-sem
nine	devyat	DAY-vyaht
ten	desyat	DAY-set

Glossary

cosmonaut   A Russian astronaut.

czar (ZAR)   A ruler of Russia before the revolution of 1917.

democracy   A form of government in which the people vote for their leaders.

geyser (GUY-zuhr)   An underground spring that shoots steam and hot water.

mortar   A heavy bowl used with a pestle for crushing things.

peninsula   A piece of land surrounded by water on three sides.

pestle   A club-shaped tool used to crush things in a mortar.

taiga (TY-guh)   A thick forest of evergreen trees.

time zone   A region in which the same time is used.

tundra   A huge area of flat, frozen land.

Fast Facts

The country of Russia covers two continents: Asia and Europe.

Moscow is the capital of Russia.

Russia is 5,000 miles (8,000 km) wide. It is 2,500 miles (4,000 km) from north to south. This is almost twice as big as the United States.

Lake Baikal, in south central Russia, is the deepest freshwater lake in the world. It is more than a mile (1.6 km) deep.

The Russian flag is made up of three wide stripes: white, blue, and red. The white stripe stands for goodness and openness. The blue stripe stands for honesty and faithfulness to the country. The red stripe stands for courage, generosity, and love.

Russia's official name is the Russian Federation. It is a democracy.

Russia's main religion is Russian Orthodox, a branch of Christianity.

The ruble is Russia's form of money. In 2003, you could get 30 rubles for one U.S. dollar.

Mount Elbrus is Russia's highest mountain. It is 18,465 feet (5,628 m) high.

The brown bear is Russia's national animal.

Soccer is the most popular sport in Russia. Russians rarely miss a soccer match!

As of July 2002, 144,978,573 people lived in Russia.

Proud to Be Russian

Yuri Gagarin (1934–1968)

Yuri Gagarin was the first man in space. He was born on a farm west of Moscow. Gagarin began training to become a *cosmonaut* after graduating from the Soviet Air Force. At the time, Russia was part of the Soviet Union. On April 12, 1961, the *Vostok 1* spacecraft carried Gagarin into orbit. The flight lasted 108 minutes. Gagarin traveled 203 miles (327 km) above Earth at speeds up to 17,000 miles (27,400 km) per hour. Gagarin died in a military plane crash in 1968. His hometown was renamed Gagarin City. Statues honoring him can be found there and in Moscow, in Yuri Gagarin Square. In addition, a crater on the Moon is named for him.

Mikhail Gorbachev (1931–   )

Mikhail Gorbachev was the last leader of the Soviet Union. Born in southwestern Russia, Gorbachev had various jobs in the government.

He became the leader of the Soviet Union in 1985. Gorbachev worked to make the country more free and democratic. Because of his efforts, countries that had been made part of the Soviet Union declared their independence. By the end of 1991, the Soviet Union broke apart and Gorbachev left office. He was named *Time* magazine's Man of the Year (1988) and Man of the Decade (1990). He also won the Nobel Peace Prize in 1990. Today, he lives near Moscow.

Anna Pavlova (1881–1931)

Anna Pavlova was one of the greatest ballerinas in history. She inspired thousands of people throughout the world to perform ballet. Pavlova was born in St. Petersburg in 1881. She entered a famous ballet school at age ten. After she graduated from the school in 1902, she traveled the world to dance. People loved her. Pavlova formed her own ballet company in 1910. She made the first of many tours to the United States. During the next fifteen years, she traveled 300,000 miles (483,000 km) and gave 4,000 dazzling performances. In 1931, Pavlova caught pneumonia. She could have been saved with an operation. The operation would have damaged her ribs, however, and left her unable to dance. Pavlova refused to give up ballet, and died at the age of fifty.

Find Out More

Books

Eyewitness Books: Russia by Kathleen Berton Murrell. DK Publishing, New York, 2000.

Russian Fairy Tales by Gillian Avery. Everyman's Library, New York, 1995.

Russia by Bob Italia. Abdo Publishing, Minneapolis, MN, 2001.

The People of Russia and Their Food by Ann L. Burckhardt. Bridgestone Books, Mankato, MN, 1996.

Web Sites

Take a virtual tour of the Hermitage Museum at **www.hermitage.ru**. The site includes color photos, the history of the museum, and information about museum education programs for children.

Go to **www.russianembassy.org** for information, news, Russian food, and more, presented by the Russian embassy.

Video

Visit **www.nationalgeographic.com** and click on the Shop link for a variety of videos about Russia, Siberia, and more.

Index

Page numbers for illustrations are in **boldface.**

About the Author

Sarah De Capua is the author of many books, including nonfiction, biographies, geography, and historical titles. She loves to travel and write about the places she has visited when she gets home. Born and raised in Connecticut, she now calls Colorado home.

Acknowledgments

My thanks to Tatiana Belykh for her generous help and contributions. *Spasiebo!*